THE AMERICAN POETRY REVIEW/HONICKMAN
FIRST BOOK PRIZE

The Honickman Foundation is dedicated to the support of projects that promote spiritual growth and creativity, education and social change. At the heart of the mission of the Honickman Foundation is the belief that creativity enriches contemporary society because the arts are powerful tools for enlightenment, equity and empowerment, and must be encouraged to effect social change as well as personal growth. A current focus is on the particular power of photography and poetry to reflect and interpret reality, and, hence, to illuminate all that is true.

The annual American Poetry Review/Honickman First Book Prize offers publication of a book of poems, a $3,000 award, and distribution by Copper Canyon Press through Consortium. Each year a distinguished poet is chosen to judge the prize and write an introduction to the winning book. The purpose of the prize is to encourage excellence in poetry, and to provide a wide readership for a deserving first book of poems. *Nine Acres* is the fourteenth book in the series.

NINE ACRES

Nine Acres

Nathaniel Perry

WINNER OF THE APR/HONICKMAN
FIRST BOOK PRIZE

The American Poetry Review
Philadelphia

Cover art: Laura Hudson, *Broadbeans*
Book design and composition: Valerie Brewster, Scribe Typography

Distribution by Copper Canyon Press/Consortium.

Library of Congress Control Number:

ISBN 978-0-9833008-1-6 (cloth, alk. paper)
ISBN 978-0-9833008-0-9 (pbk., alk. paper)

9 8 7 6 5 4 3 2 FIRST EDITION

for Kate

Contents

Introduction

I read the first poem in Nathaniel Perry's *Nine Acres* and heard a voice so clear and sane and alive in the world that I relaxed. Then I read the second, then the third — then turned to the fourth, then flipped through the pages. When I saw that all the poems in this volume were the same length, each written in meter and rhyme, I was, at first, appalled.

Then I came to understand that the poems were like furrows in a field, the constraints of form as necessary as water or sunlight. Because this is a book that concerns itself with freedom and constraint, with what we used to call husbandry — care of the land, of animals, (of a marriage, of children). *Nine Acres* speaks of the responsibilities of love.

Nathaniel Perry has made good use of an old book as a true primer and frame. He relies on the chapter titles of *Five Acres and Independence* by M.G. Kains for the marvelous titles of his poems. "Re-making a Neglected Orchard," "Water Supply," "Weeds," "Manures," "Bees," "Tools," and "Tried and True Ways to Fail" are some of my favorites. You might feel the presence of Frost here, and he's here all right; the poems shift and sidle and change their minds, then turn back again. But these poems are written from the 21st century: the neighbor beyond the wall has a name, chemicals enrich the fields he works, and the family farm is failing. Some things however remain the same, as when we lived in the dark — the elemental dark some of us can almost remember and most of us still fear. The door in the woods opens and closes as it always did. The animals, after gazing at us for a moment, turn away.

It's difficult to speak of character in art. Art will have its way with us. But reading these poems, I felt the character of the writer, his respect for the contracts we make in our lives. And I felt his love for the hard work of language so wrought as to be almost adequate to life. These poems restore and re-fresh — they taste of water and metal, arising from a spring close to the source.

Marie Howe

One of the most profitable habits you can form is systematically, every day, to go over at least part of your premises in a leisurely, scrutinizingly thoughtful way, and the whole of it at least once each week throughout the year to reap the harvest of a quiet eye and fill the granary of your mind with knowledge of the habits of helpful and harmful animals, birds and insects; to observe and understand the characteristics of plant growth from the sprouting of the seed through all the stages of stem, leaf, flower, fruit and seed development; to note and interpret the behavior of plants, poultry and animals under varying conditions of heat and cold, sunshine and shade, drouth and wetness, fair weather and foul, rich and poor feeding. Here is not only the best farm school in which to learn the duties you owe your dependants (plants and animals) and yourself for your own best interests, but in which to enjoy the most delightful compensations of farm life; for it gives the thinking observer mastery over his business, brings him *en rapport* with his environment and in tune with The Infinite.

M.G. KAINS, *Five Acres and Independence*

Introduction

I'll start this with an ending, or something
like an ending, at least there's tension and fading
light. In the back field, our neighbor
Lee's long field behind us, we were sliding

along the muddy pasture road
— the dogs, the boy and I all out
for a walk at dusk — when a coyote,
bright as tomorrow, opened and shut

and opened again the woods' dark doors
then stilled to stand and look at us.
The dogs trembled and communicated
with a quickening of every muscle

while I tried just to read the animal's
face. But all I got was the starkness
of form: that which hunts before me,
that which is not dark in the darkness.

The Farm to Choose

Where the gravel easement straightens out
into the swale they say is there
to hide a spring that only shows
its face in the strongest rains, where

the rise rises up to what
we will refer to as the meadow,
or future orchard, where the woods
reach out along the drive their shadows

to us and to the meadow, where
the driveway turns again, now hard,
beside what soon will be the garden
once we educate the yard

from being yard to being soil,
where the house, in a high place, stands
with its young eyes, I think from here
I can make out sure signs of land.

Vegetable Crops to Avoid and to Choose

We need the right varieties,
spring shell peas for half-full sun,
the long "breakfast" radishes
that grow well here and on your tongue

sparkle like spun light, potatoes
we can dig when they are new.
When we were new, or smaller-hearted,
we did not care at all for the few

things that matter to us now.
I'm still learning what that's to do
with this catalog of seeds we're pacing
through, but if someone knows, it's you,

you who have traced such lines in the garden,
you I follow with all my eyes;
we'll get the carrots right this year,
we'll tend to the baby when he cries.

Poultry

Red Star, Black Star, Golden Comet,
Buttercup, Buckeye, Delaware.
Wyandotte, Orpington, Plymouth Rock,
Cochin, Lamona, Chantecler

and Crevecouer and black-tailed banty,
Leghorn, Phoenix — buff and red,
Malay, Sultan, Sussex and Jersey
Giant. I could go on but instead

will not give in to just this language
and all its smaller charms today.
I need the eggs for breakfast, so how
about we make a deal and say

I'll give in to the eggs and then
the hens as we play our little game:
my ducking in the coop, their calling
softly out my singular name.

Essential Factors of Production

I'll make a dirty joke, you'll cringe,
but maybe later acquiesce.
The seedlings spread beneath our lights
will slowly draw their backwards breaths.

The peas are in before the rain.
It's cold, but they don't mind the cold
so much. I know you hate this rain,
frigid on your hands, but fold

the empty envelopes of seed
with satisfaction nonetheless.
The ground shows little of what we've done,
but insignificance, I guess,

is still a signal of some kind;
our secrets, hidden and so unharmed,
we're sure will soon transform us, or will
at least return to us transformed.

Re-making a Neglected Orchard

It was a good idea, cutting away
the vines and ivy, trimming back
the chest-high thicket lazy years
had let grow here. Though it wasn't for lack

of love for the trees, I'd like to point out.
Years love trees in a way we can't
imagine. They just don't use the fruit
like us; they want instead the slant

of sun through narrow branches, the buckshot
of rain on these old cherries. And we,
now that I think on it, want those
things too, we just always and desperately

want the sugar of the fruit, the best
we'll get from this irascible land:
a sweetness we can gather for years,
new stains staining the stains on our hands.

Soil Surface Management

I spent the afternoon breaking
ground. The tiller bucked and groaned
at the job, but with each pass I saw
a perfect blankness; I'd been loaned

a second life in which to grow
a third. The sun sat on its porch
and smiled. I wondered if the dirt
would be enough, a kind of torch

to set inside our lives to say,
we'll grow our food like this, our plans
will look like this — like soil squared
and measured into beds by a man

sweating through his shirt with effort.
In dirt is one life we can choose
to make. I spent the afternoon
breaking what I *knew* we'd use.

Lay and Lay-out of Land

We go to bed early — you
sometimes earlier than me.
The baby wakes us only once
we hope in the night, in the waveless sea,

the surfaceless sea that is night for us.
When the moon is wide I watch the garden
by its light. And I am frailer here
in the light; the sprouts and greens are hardened

to the keener darker cold. My shadow
is infinitely smaller than white
pines in blue light, and I'll join you
soon in bed. The morning will fight

its way into our room again,
and you will stir and I will stir.
When the sun sails through the maples, it's always
never been so bright before.

Where to Locate

The sound of a busy road just makes
you crazy, you said, though not van-lights-
across-the-wall crazy as they come
up the drive to take us away in the night —

like the time I dreamt a sickness took you
from me, ambulance-flicker across
those same walls like fireworks outside,
crickets singing brightly of loss

in the sirenless night as I dreamed I watched
you disappear into the lights
and then down the road. There is a road
here, but it's quiet as a kite.

It rises and falls with the land, and we
rise with it, also like a kite,
in a wind we had no hand in choosing,
but trust, looking down, one day, we might.

Functions of Water

On rainy days the place seems smaller,
acres still ringed and shrouded by trees,
but the sky is closer, like something landing.
I know you'd like to ask me — please

can we go inside, it's cold, I'm cold,
the baby's cold — but you know I won't
let you go inside yet. The boy is shrieking
as if the colors behind and in front

of his new eyes are all too much
to take in at once, too much joy
at once, I mean. But I called you out
here for this early rain. The boy

can see what he needs to. I need you here,
beside me, to see this place filled
by something that is not us, our every
acre ringed and shrouded and still.

Drainage

A stranger came to the door last night;
you were scared you said, or we were scared,
you corrected yourself, including the dogs
and baby in your story. Unfair,

you insisted, for a man to walk
up to a house so all alone,
so far up in these fields when someone
else inside might be alone

as well, or not so well, but scared.
You whispered to our bigger dog
to bark and send the man away
and praised the dog. Through the lit fog

of night glass, you did not know the man
who didn't show his face. And, no,
the stranger wasn't me, but worse,
someone even I do not know.

Tried and True Ways to Fail

Cut the tree with a bent bow saw.
When the blade bucks and sticks in the heart
of the fallen pine, try to free
it with your gloveless hand. Seek art

in the wind's wrestling the trees. Decide
what your children will think about something,
like difficult art up in the pines.
Or imagine them always happy and running.

Brace your strength with a foot on the trunk
to the left of the buried blade; pull
with everything in you. When you fall,
unbalanced, notice the maples are full

of color — or filling up, like a glass
of water. Everything you can see
is filling or full. The boy is starting
to crawl. The saw is still in the tree.

Lime

I'm spreading lime on our smaller garden
knowing it won't have any real
effect this year (soil paces
and waits and only slowly steals

what it needs). God I hate waiting
and doing and doing for tomorrow
—only liars find it satisfying.
What paths could possibly look more narrow

than those I see etched out behind me
as I walk spreading lime on our field? Which
footprint was the first one I made
when I started? The sun has shifted, unstitches

the shadows it made all afternoon.
I'm lost in the pattern of walking this field,
where nothing grows the same each year,
though even that is a kind of yield.

Green Manures and Cover Crops

Is there a center in all of this,
or only field peas in flower, or just
our meadow peas in flower? Yes,
all of it, and they, as they must

be, are only ours, and you
are only mine, and, of course, ours
as well, which is the same as mine
for now, while we are undevoured,

which will not last and will not last
because it seems it will until
the evening ends exactly as
it ended here tonight — still,

with light in the trees and storms somewhere
out towards Prospect — which is to say
forever. But stay with me like peas
in the meadow, which is to say always.

Bush and Cane Fruits

This rain will fall all day. The boy
and I are watching it fill the fields,
which is good for fields. To fill, to feel
filled will last and be a shield

against the vacant weeks, the drier
days. And what are the things that fill
us up? Little graces, good food,
the arrows we trade, our small good will?

We don't know what saves us. Better to be
a field, the boy and I decide,
at least he seems to agree. He's filling
a bucket with everything he finds,

and he's so pleased when it is full,
his smile a clutch of raspberries
in the forest sun — no more worries,
no more to do, nothing's scary.

Fruit Tree Pruning

The time to prune, my little book says,
is when the tools are sharp, an old
joke, I'm sure, but I'm not so sure
what it means as advice, practical

or otherwise. Should we love each other
only at our loveliest, or speak
of stars just on the darkest nights?
Regardless, the wind outside is leaking

through the trees, a low ocean
sound: incessant, not ceasing, unceased.
I'm reading my book at the prow of a storm,
a spring night howler, a small release

of energies not my own, not my slow
increases, my fumbling towards fruit
beneath unimpressed stars. The time to prune,
I'd say, is when you can make the cut.

Tools

My hands for pulling grass around
the carrots. A blade for poplar seedlings
that shouldn't have seeded here. My foot
for pokeweed and the pleasure of weeding

something with a single kick.
A pen-knife for a splinter. Our bodies
for comfort. The first days of squash to fill
us with summer. Beets for comfort, your body,

cool in the June evening, for that,
for that coolness, which is comfort. Stakes
to reign in the nightshades. The coming rain
for rain. The boy to laugh and make

me chase him from the garden. The garden
for the moon to find. This land for work
which makes us whole, which holds for us
the days and holds away the dark.

Farm Finance

Next door, or not next door — all
we share is a field and a rutted road —
I hear Lee this morning hitching up
his tractor, the diesel yawn, and a load

of silage clanking across the field
headed for another field.
He told me they lost the place once
in the thirties — the cows, the work, the yield

not enough even to pay taxes.
Lee wasn't there to see it, not born
of course, but the family bought it back,
fields and field-roads all still worn

with the ruts they'd made. The place is still
unchanged by years: the hills, the swaying
wheat, the carts of rot, and the kind
of debt that Lee is out there paying.

Irrigation

If there's any elegance in life
it's in the way that water runs
from sky to spring and spring to field,
from field to field just for the fun

of it, or for the fullness of it
— a glut of needless elegance,
the thoughtless pooling up of pools
along the drive, the maintenance

of balance at the edges of
the pools, and of the field I suppose,
though that is a different kind of balance,
one that I maintain, in rows.

And speaking of balance, I lost mine today
in the earlier rain, leaning to weed
the carrots. I went down wet and empty-
handed, inelegant as need.

City vs. Country Life

I envy those who know precisely
what to do or where to live
or how: the dog sleeps under the bed,
mice in the weeds, bees in their hives —

though I've not seen a hive around
here, just blocks of quiet wasps
in their condominiums. The blues
of their bodies are difficult to grasp,

knives of darkened light. I have
to kill them, of course, exterminate
the word we use, but let's not pity
the wasp this impermanence, not hate

ourselves for moving to his country.
He sleeps his sleep where he chooses,
country or city, his blue (now
I see it) the color of our bruises.

Cropping Systems

Lee stopped his putting feed corn in
to tell me that his father died.
He said the place didn't really seem
like much of a farm anymore, his shy

face not shy in the evening sun
or in the grief still warm in him.
He came down from the tractor while
we talked it over, cut the engine

to hear me better — though I didn't
have much to say that wasn't already
clear in the slow stretch of oats
and meadow behind us. The sun restudied

our bodies in shadow as we turned away
from dying and spoke of hay and drought,
as if to say that's all we ever
really know anything about.

Essentials of Spraying and Dusting

Lee's putting poison on his corn.
Though I'd never raise the issue, I try
not to think what else is in his creek
besides the chapel light of high

morning sun and hoof prints from the deer
and jailbreak cows and my dogs, lost
in the wildness of wild water. Lee
is putting poison on maybe his last

year of corn — he told me he can't
farm it alone anymore, one man
on a tractor not antagonist
enough to manage this greening canvas.

Lee's putting poison on his corn,
his daddy put poison on the corn.
And it grew! So many things, so many
things in us when we are born.

Something to Sell Every Day

I can see our potatoes in flower from here,
wind-bent then lifted, confused, the way
your hands move when you try to explain
the field you saw that moved you, gray

light today still strong enough
to give shadow to the buckwheat set,
after the season's first cut, around
the field at the baler's whim. Yet

there seemed a pattern to you, jogging
by this morning, your footsteps marking
out their own pattern in the air,
which the killdeer could hear, which the barking

jays could hear, which the knot of sparrows
in the windbreak could hear, but would not betray
— so what, then, is meaning? You move
your hands one way, then the other way.

Water Supply

The winter squash is spread around
the field. It's just up with this last
rain, which makes us glad to be
creatures of water, of sluices, of fast

drainage. The rain divides and rivers
through our gutters and fields, to our seeds
and to the crops which have already
found their flowers, and to the weeds

which have found their flowers. You and I
can hear the water as we fall
asleep — some angle of the roof
allows for constant chatter. All

I do all night is half-listen
to see if it is still raining,
the other half of both of us
dreaming what the squash is dreaming.

Weeds

I told you I was worried. Water
had collected up against the foundation
from the rain we had, and you must have thought
I was talking about *our* foundation,

though I meant, of course, the one beneath
the house. But it was too late, your mood
had changed and then my mood was changed,
and we charged around the house mooding

and changing. I siphoned the water
away from the house, which took a while,
which was probably good. You made dinner,
which was good, and also took a while.

As we ate, the sun drew familiar
shapes on our walls, but we didn't notice.
And then the light slipped down and made
a bright new shape, but we didn't notice.

Compost

Desire is what we make of it;
new stretch of soil, old patch of soil.
We want more food so add a row
and scare-strips made from aluminum foil

hung from the lowest branches of trees
nearby and coathangers stabbed in the ground.
Deer approach and shy away
with a slight sound, a slippery sound

like the sun, if it made one, as it closes days.
But the sun is silent, as frightened birds
are so almost silent, which is exactly
what we want — soft fleeing, like words

that slowly leave us. The sun in the garden
says it, for one, won't leave us yet;
it's not that we get what we want exactly,
but that want, if we want it, is all we get.

Coldframes and Hotbeds

Staring at you squatting down
among the lettuces, I can't
help but imagine you naked there,
the sun and summer having lent

your skin their shimmer, desire a sun-
flower opening and turning
me always towards your sweat and body.
I probably shouldn't say I'm burning

for you, or sing of the lines that sweat
so ably traces down your chest,
or of the okra stalk's soft bloom
my mind keeps returning to. No, the best

I can do is avoid cliché and take you
by the hand; I'll lay you down
beside the coldframe we built last year
to warm this garden's winter ground.

Plants for Sale

Moon in the clear-cut, the neighbor's acres;
I'm trespassing to explore the light.
Night birds call and call and I get
to where I can't split out what's right

beside me and what's in the still-standing
trees, what sort of spirit's come
to visit me, or at least to visit
this place. And if the dead do run

among us, it'd be in a dark like this —
one not really dark at all,
the just-full moon so ripe you'd keep
it in a jar if you could. The small

growth, shy in this wasted place
(cut for little money and pulp wood),
clutches the bright ground; nothing
reborn is really understood.

Soils and their Care

The field we bought is filled with clover.
You are still my lover, I am still
yours. Our children are halfway here,
and we try to imagine being filled

more — like a pint of beer before
it loaves above the glass and kisses
the landlord's hand. Remember the year
we lived in London? We don't miss

it much, but you were my lover there
as well, and I was yours, which was
a good way to be in the city, so many
roads to cross and places to puzzle

over. And what, exactly, binds
this August meadow and that year?
I could say love — we'd all, of course,
expect that. I should, but won't, say fear.

Small Farm Fruit Gardens

This night withholds the things it knows;
its light is only make-up, costume
or apology, however you choose to see it.
Fruit trees ascetic in the rooms

their shadows build for them, fields
stretched and smoothed by the moon's quiet hand
as it slips below the tree line, I
am left in shadow's shadows to stand

too still and figure all the turnings
turning us, or where we'll turn
now the good light's left us, crawled around
behind our backs like the copper urns

of beetles dropping forever into
the cherry's branches. Come back little moon —
dark night's noon, heaven-raker,
cloister-maker, buttonhole, bloom.

Bees

One of the dogs unearthed a pile
of yellow jackets in the ground.
I was with the boy in the woods, teaching
him words (woodsorrel, finch) and what sounds

the wind can make when we heard a rush
like blackbirds riding their Ferris wheels
up and through the trees, except
it wasn't in the trees. I could feel,

also, my feet hum a little,
and then the dog was running, a small
madness of bees boiling up
from the dug-up ground. All in all,

I was still reminded of blackbirds — strange
indebtedness of movement, the mantling
of portent. But with bees you run, and we ran,
all likenesses to birds notwithstanding.

Renting vs. Buying

Two people I didn't know today
were hunting arrowheads in the field
behind us. I heard them, and the dogs
heard them, chased their truck stealing

along the path back there. I took
the boy to meet them and to collect
the dogs. They told me their names, Lena
and Mike, and Mike, beaming with sweat

and September, showed me the flint-head
he'd just turned up — the best he'd found
in years, he said. It was the gray
of something dead, the gray of the sound

of thunder, and hammered so all over
it seemed not stone but purely arrow.
It was small and dull in my hand, but Mike
said it had glittered in the furrow.

Greenhouses

The sun comes up like a sunrise somewhere
else, and, still foreign, finds a way
into windows, door seams, half-dreams, minds' eyes.
Out of our smallish comforts, we wake.

It's cool this morning, though I know
the air will warm like heated glass.
I'm taking the boy down to the pond,
and where the field-road turns, low grass

wet with the darkness now behind us,
an owl is calling, hunting, or only
reminding us he can condense
our moment into his. The lonely

sound is not lonely. Light is more
than light — though the sun, at least, by now
is familiar and setting the trees on familiar
fire, or a fire we've come to know.

Who is Likely to Succeed?

I always assumed beginnings were
the best places to start. But times
are that middles are all you see
or something slowly muddles the line

between starts and middles or middles and ends,
like love, or something just like love
but more so for its having lit
the corners of what you'd always thought of

as the start of something but now
seems exactly like the middle
of something else, a thing you had thought
you might miss, like the sweet note on a fiddle,

if you'd tried. And now my song's all soured
with thinking. I'll start over. It begins:
you, then you, then here, where the trees
are bright, will soften, will brighten again.

Seeds and Seeding

We're shaking seeds into their furrows
and wonder how they stay asleep
for years. The clouds this afternoon
are heavy poke-sacks, flocks of deep

pockets swollen black and full
of rain. The night will fill with waking —
children staring at the thunder
in the ceiling, nightbirds shrilling and staking

their claims in the longer calms, bush beans,
a second row of beets, beginning
to unsleep; the rain, the wildness, doing
and undoing, slow hands unpinning

night from the background, like a flag
meant for a ceremony where the part
we're meant to play is a mystery,
and everything is about to start.

Manures

I'll say it again, it will piss you off
again. I'll do it again, it will make
you cry again. I know I'll chase
the dogs again and scream and shake

them when I find them. I'll promise later
to understand again that they
are animals. I'll try again
to figure exactly when it's safe

for me to be an animal.
I'll piss you off, and you'll say it again.
I'll start to cry, and you'll do what you did
again. The storm watch will begin

with thunder. The thunder will begin
with animals taking cover. Take cover
sweetheart, little heart, this too will accrete,
will build and repeat and then start over.

Storage of Fruits and Vegetables

Well, the melons didn't grow
as big as you would've liked them to.
The corn made ears the size of those giant
pencils you get as a kid, which it's true

are big for pencils, but for corn
not what we'd imagined exactly.
Lee made fun of me a little,
his acres of corn waving calmly

in the sun — but our potatoes came in
like gold, like loaves of buried bread;
beans are canned and stacked inside
like numbers in a table. The dead

are still dead, I'm afraid, but we've tried. We try
to live off this life nonetheless. Look up —
our beans have reached the tops of the poles
I set in the ground, and they will not stop.

Selection of Tree Fruits

Hay light — the ripened light of evening
at baling time, third cut, late
September — makes songs with what
it finds, as if it were not weighted

with autumn's burden, which is, I'll admit,
all we want right now. We're sick of green,
of weeds reseeding, lurid pokeberries
bunched and fat. The season's mean

with an open, metaphorical
kind of discipline. The walnuts are thick
with walnuts, but stripped by wind of leaves.
Persimmons soften for our sake.

I'll strain them for their pulp when they
are almost rotten; we'll celebrate
the sweetness of decline — fall's little
ditty, where mercy rhymes with fate.

Frost Damage Prevention

I think we get angry every time
the same things happen. Our old fights
float down from the same events the way
frost bows autumn beans in the night

no matter how early we cover them.
I don't know if wind smuggles in
the ice which crusts their stalks at dawn,
or if the fact of frost has been

forever inside them, like maggots in meat,
and rises to the surface when called
there by an alchemist moon, or if
night birds, will and widow, all

gather there in that cove in prayer
to anoint the plants with holy water.
It doesn't really matter though;
that we're again defeated matters.

Farm Accounts

for AN

The hill on Lee's place is the highest
here. On clear mornings I'll sometimes
find myself above even
the vultures, whose narrowing circles rhyme

always and always with death. I can see
their backs shimmer in the ploughshare
sun. Today I took to the hill
a special sadness, thinking there

of your closer death and, of course, the brighter
thing you've left for us to hold
a while. When I turned at the top of the road,
I saw Lee below disking the cold

fields for fall, and I saw a hawk,
morning-hunting, diving, his eye
fixed on some small life, which he took,
but which with him rose again to the sky.

Live Stock

In windrows, sun-dark thickets, a flush
of wings seems simple, like fear, or love,
and ends, at least for now, my waiting
for the shadow of, the sound of.

Thrushes, in handfuls, candle up
into the pines and ask what wonder
I thought it was I wanted. Trees
crossing in the air? The thunder

of wind in their long hair? I like
how you can hear the wind coming
from the thick oak woods down the hill
to here — like something slowly running.

It's comforting, to know when a thing
is on its way — not like the fear
of closer quicker sounds, sure signs
of the other animals out here.

Sewage Disposal

There's a pair of wood ducks at the pond.
They scare away each time I turn
the corner to the berm that holds
the water back from the woods. I've learned

at least that when I yell at them
to stay — their flight already past
begun, their backs and scoldings soaked
with morning sun — there is a lasting

echo: *wait, wait, wait...*
But it's always too late. I guess I've never
seen them in an honest sense,
if honesty is our endeavor

here, though I'm not sure that's all
we're good for, to flush and call after our shames.
What could I admit to the ducks,
the pond, that wouldn't come back the same?

Grapes

We're not growing them yet; we didn't
have time this year. Though I have ideas
for an arbor in my head — the plans
are in my head, I mean, what idiot

would put an arbor in his head?
Arbors are best in the afternoon sun,
where foresight and angle become a shade
to sit in, when the angel buntings

flair their incredible blue in the grasses,
and you really can't believe it. Who could?
— shade darker than memory,
arbor standing where you stood

to build it. In your head, in mine,
is nothing but sky and ocean, no right
thing to build an arbor on,
to vine our heavy days and nights.

Strawberries

Matted row, plant in fall
or spring — watch the sun, frost
in early April. Little hearts,
little heart, I thought that you were lost

in setting out the slips, but you
were lost instead in the dove-song
caroling from our stand of sweetgum.
Nothing wrong, nothing wrong, and nothing's wrong

in this moment, which makes a moment
good, and is rare, which is also maybe
good. I know in another moment
you'll think again about the baby

we thought we'd lost, but somehow still
is singing to us from its gum-tree.
Like fear, our strawberries will bloom
in promise, a riotous decree.

How to Avoid Nursery Stock Losses

Don't walk too far or fast; don't help,
though you'll want to, with the autumn seeding,
don't bend to check the watermelons.
Worry, of course, about the bleeding.

Try not to hold the one we have
— he's heavier, more dangerous
by the day — though he won't understand
the tremor in your hands, the crush

of worry in your hands. Don't think
about it, at least when you're not already
thinking about it. Your body is
not yours, so worry about the steady

pulse of dread that you can't keep
from checking: who's there? who's there? Don't start
to count the silences instead
of the softer footsteps of the heart.

Figures Don't Lie

Nights, we notice the field hinged
to stars, or to the field the stars
are set on. In our earthly field,
hay is still baled and waiting far

in the distance, and so I say the stars
are fire baled. But who has reaped
them? What or who will they feed?
The tractor's not fit to move them; seeping

heavy through the tines they soak
back up to the sky. The mind can't move
them either, they get trapped inside
and rattle there and scratch deep grooves

there. Resigned, we always, at least,
find the few patterns we know before
we turn away — sisters, a swan,
little bear, warrior and sword.

Commercial Fertilizers

Rain done, moon out, I want to walk
down to Lee's creek to hear it strain
against its rocks, to see the pools
— no, sudden ponds; no, tamer oceans —

cover so completely where
I every morning cross. I know
in this bright-starred darkness after rain
there is no footpath there. And so

the thinking stars arranged above
this house would say that by transference
there is no footpath here either:
I will not go to the creek. What chance

did I have? You can be fed too much
of beauty, of moon shards, the dense sorrows
of a creek that won't be crossed. One
in seven nights I will lie fallow.

Wind Breaks, Pro and Con

I could barely hear you over the roar
of it in my ears, in the trees, the grass,
the leaves on the ground. It's everywhere,
you said, pushing us, unmassing

the air, shaking the house. What is?
I asked, do you mean the wind? You said
you couldn't hear, so mouthed to me
all that again about the leaden

crashing at our backs at the crest
of the wide field, and that thing about
mass you said again too. Or did
you say unmasted? I started to shout.

You just repeated, everywhere, everywhere
— a warning maybe, a sound like bells
in fog. But did you mean the wind?
Did you mean this wind or something else?

Capital

December, sunlight stretched, Christmas
music across the radio;
a downy woodpecker in the dogwood
pauses at the stations he knows.

He's long in the grasp of our window,
the tree so close to the house it must
have been spared when the back lot was cleared
in a nod to beauty or the rust-

bellied bluebirds forever stopping
there. Rache is running through
the year's long branches of light that yawn
across our floor, and something's new,

a lodestone in us, or capital
hidden in our ledger: a joy,
a little drummer rocking around
the dogwood, or just a little boy.

Transplanting

for SRS

The wind is an animal in the trees,
or trees reanimate the wind.
An animal hides like wind in trees;
trees are the spirit hide of wind.

When I first heard the tree-wind (the wind-trees?),
I did think it was an animal
— something nameless that shouldn't be there,
or should, but not in daylight, this full

January sun, which is
a kind of animal itself,
the way it shocks the naked trees
it lights — and I thought perhaps the gulf

between the woods and our small bodies
might narrow. But then I knew the nameless
animal would know me, so I begged it:
animal, animus, name us, name us.

Grafting Fruit Trees

You've always liked to hold my hand.
I'll spare us both the metaphors
and parsings of the gesture — how it is
so just like balance, a crutch, a shore

and sea, a strangeing trick, rootstock
in a nursery. Though now you could complain
I haven't spared us after all
and cheapened, by trying to explain,

a thing that needed only pointing
to. I'll try again. You've always
liked to hold my hand. I've always
liked to try not to look sideways

at you when you balance in
my hand. Two idiots in love.
But fruit still fills our sudden branches,
the wind still what makes us move.

The Farm Library

In my copy of M.G. Kains'
Five Acres and Independence,
a 1970s reprint of
the 1940s' making sense

of the "obsolescence" of the first printing
from 1935, a once final
chapter, "The Farm Library," is
omitted but for the ghost of its title

on the copyright page, which duly explains
the surgery almost as if
the revelation itself was a new
kind of pain. What did Kains, his skiff

of a book shored up, his harvest stored
for winter, need me to know of knowledge?
That in seed and land we find an anchor,
and in language we weigh out our courage.

Acknowledgments

American Poetry Review: "Introduction," "Tried and True Ways to Fail," "Farm Finance," "Compost," "Figures Don't Lie," and "The Farm Library"

Beloit Poetry Journal: "Seeds and Seeding"

The Common: "Functions of Water"

The Gettysburg Review: "The Farm to Choose," "Poultry," "Drainage," and "Remaking a Neglected Orchard"

Virginia Foundation for the Humanities (Tough Times Companion): "Farm Accounts"

Acknowledgment should also be made to the editors of *Poetry Daily, Verse Daily,* and The Poetry Foundation's *American Life in Poetry* project for re-printing some of these poems.

Many thanks to Terry Morgan, Susan Welsand and Lee Amos for living their ways.

Finally, I am indebted, of course, to M.G. Kains, whose classic work on small-farm management, *Five Acres and Independence* (1935), provided the nominal inspiration for this book and whose fifty-two chapter titles have been transplanted to be the titles of these fifty-two poems.